ACKNOWLEDGMENTS

The publisher would like to thank the following individuals and organizations
for providing the photographs used in this book:

Heather Angel: 47 center

Britstock-IFA/F. Aberham: 23, 40 top right, /Robert Maier: 45 left.

Bruce Coleman: 31, /George McCarthy: 35 right, /Charlie Ott: 21 center left, /Dieter & Mary Plage: 47 bottom,
/Hans Reinhard: 6 main picture, 7, /Leonard Lee Rue: 21 bottom left, /John Visser: 39,
/Rod Williams: 4 bottom right.

Frank Lane Picture Agency/J. Finch: 45 right, /Michael Gore: 14, /A. R. Hamblin: 26, /P. Heard: 4 bottom left, /David
Hosking: 25 top left, /E. & D. Hosking: 27 left, /S. Kaslowski: 29 bottom right, /M. Ranjit: 42 bottom left,
/Van Rostrand: 38, /H. Schrempp 8, /Silvestris 15 center, 16 top and bottom, 21 top, /T. Whittaker 40 bottom.

Bob Langrish 10/11 top.

NHPA/Anthony Bannister: 21 bottom right, /Stephen Dalton: 13, 25 top right, 30, /Nigel Dennis: 19 bottom,
/Gerard Lacz: 27 right, /Dave Watts: 11 bottom left, /David Woodfall: 37 bottom left.

Oxford Scientific Films/Toni Angermayer: 42 top right, /Eyal Bartov: 35 left, /Stephen Dalton: 12,
/Zigmund Leszczynski: 28, /Steve Turner: 25 bottom right.

Science Photo Library/Dr Jeremy Burgess: 20 top, /CNRI: 11 top right, /Ralph Eagle: 37 center left,
/Prof P. Motta, Dept of Anatomy, University "La Sapienza," Rome: 20 bottom, /Omikron: 25 bottom left, 29 top right.

Zefa Picture Library: 6 bottom right, 18, 37 bottom right, /J. Bernardes: 19 top.

ILLUSTRATORS:

Mike Atkinson (Garden Studio): 7 top left and bottom left, 8 left, 10, 14, 15 right, 17, 19 right,
21 top right, 22 bottom, 24 bottom, 26 bottom, 30.

John Butler: (Ian Fleming & Associates): 4, 11, 16, 43.

Miranda Gray (Maggie Mundy): title page, 12, 13 bottom, 15 left, 27 bottom, 29 bottom,
31 top, 34-35 center, 37 top, 38, 39 left, 45, 46-47 top.

Doreen McGuiness (Garden Studio): 9 main, 28 top, 41, 44, 46 bottom.

Ed Stuart: 5, 6, 7 right, 8 top right, 9 insets, 13 top, 18, 19 left, 20, 21 bottom left,
22 top right, 23, 24 top, 25, 26-27 top, 28 bottom, 29 top, 31 bottom, 32-33,
34 bottom, 35 top, 36, 37 center, 40, 43 bottom.

HAMLYN CHILDREN'S BOOKS:

Editor: Andrew Farrow
Designer: Annie Sharples
Production Controller: Linda Spillane
Picture Researcher: Anna Smith

First American edition, 1994

Library of Congress Cataloging-in-Publication Data
Parker, Steve.
Mammals / Steve Parker. — 1st American ed.
p. cm. — (Inside-outside)
Includes index.
ISBN 0-679-84919-X
1. Mammals — Juvenile literature [1. Mammals.] I. Title.
II. Series: Inside-outside (New York, N.Y.)
QL706.2.P375 1994
599—dc20   94-1595 CIP AC

Manufactured by Proost, Belgium.
1 2 3 4 5 6 7 8 9 10

CONTENTS

MAMMALS

Mammals are a group of animals that all have certain things in common. All mammals have hair, sometimes called fur. They are warm-blooded, which means that their body temperature stays the same no matter what the temperature is outside. And mammal mothers suckle, or nurse, their babies from milk glands on their bodies. Mammals also have a better developed brain than other types of animals.

WHERE DO WE COME FROM?

A long time ago there were no mammals – there were no living creatures of any kind! Our Earth was still forming, and life was not possible. Then, about 3.5 billion years ago, the first living things appeared. They were probably tiny specks of jelly, floating in the oceans. As these early creatures multiplied, a few became different. If the difference helped it survive, the newer form of life was successful. It took millions of years for the creatures we know today to gradually develop.

A well-developed brain (pages 32-33)

Lungs and a heart (pages 22-25)

External ears (page 34)

Teeth attached to a bony jaw (page 19)

The spider (above) is furry. But it has eight legs, not four, and no backbone. The pigeon (left) has warm blood, but feathers, not fur. So neither is a mammal.

INSIDE MAMMALS

Today there are about 4,000 different species, or kinds, of mammals. They come in all shapes and sizes, from tiny shrews to huge whales. And they include the most familiar mammal of all – you!

This book peers inside the mammal body to see how the many complicated parts work together like a living machine – to help the animal move, breathe, feed, grow, think, and reproduce.

WHAT IS A MAMMAL?

A typical mammal has:

Hairy or furry skin (pages 20-21) – even whales have some hair!

Milk glands for suckling (feeding) its young (pages 44-45)

Young that are born well formed (pages 44-45)

A backbone (pages 6 and 8)

"Warm blood" – the ability to maintain a stable body temperature (page 25)

Four limbs (pages 6-7 and 12-17)

DID YOU KNOW?

Most scientists believe that humans have evolved over 5 - 10 million years, from prehistoric apes. We know that an ape-like creature, *Australopithecus,* walked upright like us, more than 3 million years ago. Fossils of *Homo habilis* ("Handy human"), and then *Homo erectus* ("Upright human"), show how today's humans could have evolved.

THE EVOLUTION OF LIFE

million years ago (mya)

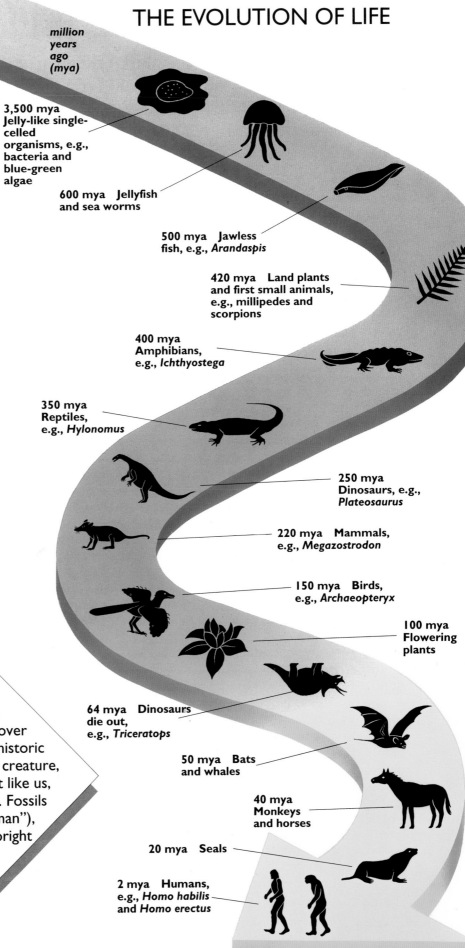

3,500 mya Jelly-like single-celled organisms, e.g., bacteria and blue-green algae

600 mya Jellyfish and sea worms

500 mya Jawless fish, e.g., *Arandaspis*

420 mya Land plants and first small animals, e.g., millipedes and scorpions

400 mya Amphibians, e.g., *Ichthyostega*

350 mya Reptiles, e.g., *Hylonomus*

250 mya Dinosaurs, e.g., *Plateosaurus*

220 mya Mammals, e.g., *Megazostrodon*

150 mya Birds, e.g., *Archaeopteryx*

100 mya Flowering plants

64 mya Dinosaurs die out, e.g., *Triceratops*

50 mya Bats and whales

40 mya Monkeys and horses

20 mya Seals

2 mya Humans, e.g., *Homo habilis* and *Homo erectus*

HOLDING UP THE JELLY

Every mammal has a skeleton that lies under the skin and muscles. Without one, a mammal would be a pile of goo. The skeleton is a framework that supports the soft parts of the body. It is made up of more than 200 bones. All mammals have roughly the same number and type of bones, but they vary in size and shape. For example, an elephant's toe bone is bigger than a shrew's whole skeleton!

The long neck of the magnificent giraffe allows it to reach high into trees to find its food.

SKULL AND SPINE

Every skeleton has the same basic design. The animal's head is protected by the skull. The skull is attached to a row of bones called vertebrae. These vertebrae make up the spinal column in the neck and back. Front limbs, or arms, are attached to the spinal column at the shoulders, and rear limbs, or legs, are attached at the hips. Some bones protect the body's soft inner parts. The ribs guard the lungs and heart, and the hipbones cradle the parts in the lower body.

Neck bone

WORKING BONES

Besides being the body's framework, the skeleton stores minerals and other substances. If an animal goes without food for a long time, some of these minerals can be used. Bone marrow, in the center of many bones, makes millions of new blood cells every day. These pour into the bloodstream to replace the cells that die.

Most mammal skeletons have 7 vertebral bones in the neck and about 12 in the chest. They also have 5 in the lower back, 4 or 5 in the hip region, and 10 or more in the tail. So a giraffe, with its enormously long neck, has 7 neck bones - and so does a mouse!

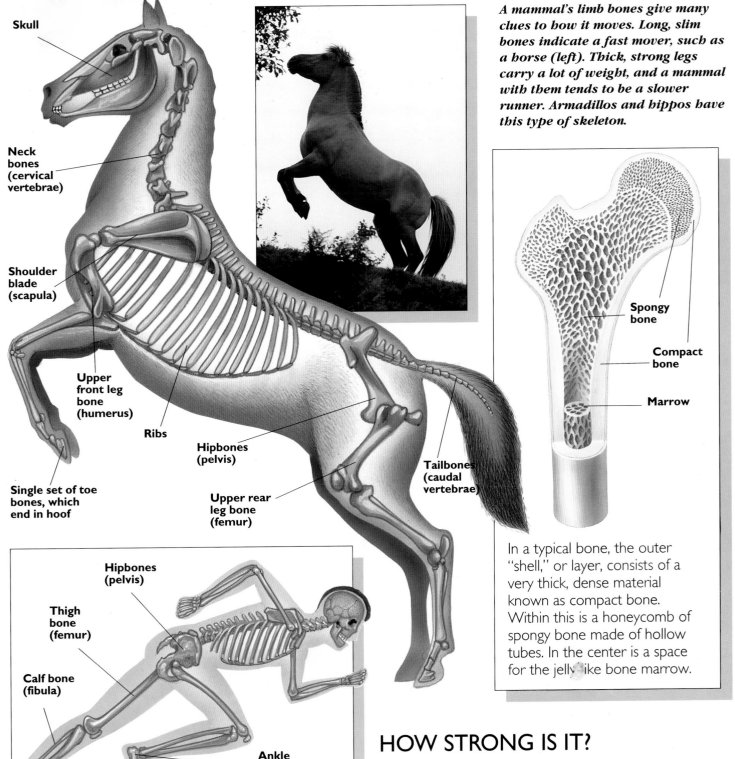

Skull

Neck
bones
(cervical
vertebrae)

Shoulder
blade
(scapula)

Upper
front leg
bone
(humerus)

Ribs

Hipbones
(pelvis)

Single set of toe
bones, which
end in hoof

Upper rear
leg bone
(femur)

Tailbones
(caudal
vertebrae)

A mammal's limb bones give many clues to how it moves. Long, slim bones indicate a fast mover, such as a horse (left). Thick, strong legs carry a lot of weight, and a mammal with them tends to be a slower runner. Armadillos and hippos have this type of skeleton.

Spongy
bone

Compact
bone

Marrow

In a typical bone, the outer "shell," or layer, consists of a very thick, dense material known as compact bone. Within this is a honeycomb of spongy bone made of hollow tubes. In the center is a space for the jelly-like bone marrow.

Hipbones
(pelvis)

Thigh
bone
(femur)

Calf bone
(fibula)

Shinbone
(tibia)

Foot bones
(metatarsals)

Ankle
bones
(tarsals)

The human skeleton has 206 bones. Humans are the only mammals that walk regularly on two feet. This way of moving, called bipedalism, has led to the leg bones becoming much longer and stronger than the arms. When running, the foot and toe bones push powerfully against the ground.

HOW STRONG IS IT?

Living bone has a blood supply to bring it oxygen and nutrients (food), and nerves to detect strain or a fracture (break) in the bone.

A typical bone is about one-third water. The other two-thirds are made of the important protein collagen, which makes the bone tough and slightly flexible, and minerals such as calcium and phosphorus for hardness and strength. The toughest bones are about as strong as reinforced concrete or cast iron – but up to five times lighter.

JOINS AND JOINTS

A skeleton with its bones fixed together would be useless. The body would be unable to move. So, where one bone attaches to another, there is a joint. Try moving the different parts of your body. Feel how the bones tilt, swing, and swivel on each other.

VERY FLEXIBLE

If bones touched each other in a joint, they would rub and scrape, and soon wear down. So where the bones meet, they are covered with a shiny, smooth, slightly softer substance called cartilage, or gristle. Cartilage can stand wear and tear much better than bone.

OIL AND STRAPS

Joints even have their own natural "oil" inside! A soft, flexible bag covers the joint. It contains a slippery liquid called synovial fluid that lubricates the joint, like oil in a car engine. Around the joint are thick, stretchy straps known as ligaments. They hold the bones near each other and keep them from pulling apart. The result is a strong joint that moves smoothly and does not wear out. It would be the envy of any car mechanic!

In the backbone, each bone can move slightly in relation to those above and below it. These small movements add up along the whole length of the spine, so the mammal can bend and twist its neck and back.

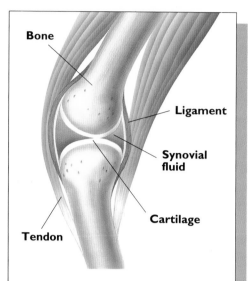

Bone

Ligament

Synovial fluid

Cartilage

Tendon

A bone is usually wider at its ends, which meet other bones in joints, than along its length. You can see this clearly in animals with long, slim legs such as giraffes and deer. The extra width spreads the weight more evenly.

Long, thin animals such as this stoat spend a great deal of time down burrows, either in their own nests or chasing prey such as rabbits. The stoat's backbone is extremely flexible, and it can even turn around in a burrow hardly wider than its body.

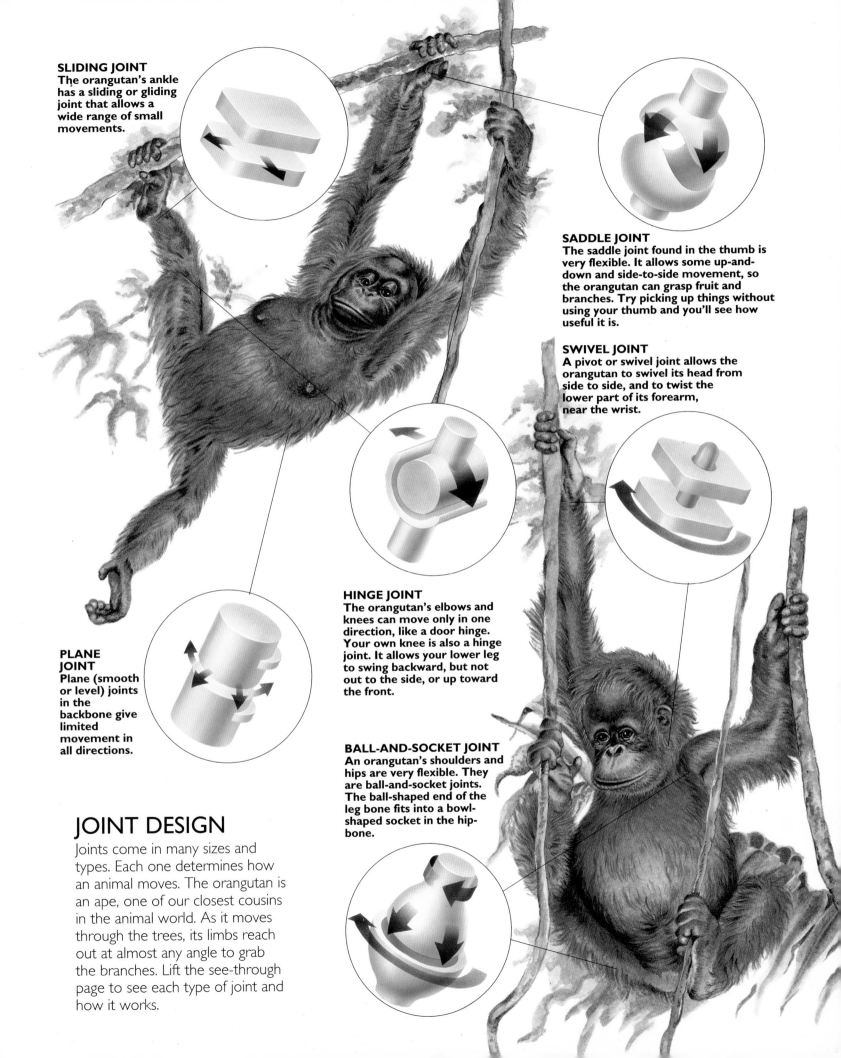

SLIDING JOINT
The orangutan's ankle has a sliding or gliding joint that allows a wide range of small movements.

SADDLE JOINT
The saddle joint found in the thumb is very flexible. It allows some up-and-down and side-to-side movement, so the orangutan can grasp fruit and branches. Try picking up things without using your thumb and you'll see how useful it is.

SWIVEL JOINT
A pivot or swivel joint allows the orangutan to swivel its head from side to side, and to twist the lower part of its forearm, near the wrist.

PLANE JOINT
Plane (smooth or level) joints in the backbone give limited movement in all directions.

HINGE JOINT
The orangutan's elbows and knees can move only in one direction, like a door hinge. Your own knee is also a hinge joint. It allows your lower leg to swing backward, but not out to the side, or up toward the front.

BALL-AND-SOCKET JOINT
An orangutan's shoulders and hips are very flexible. They are ball-and-socket joints. The ball-shaped end of the leg bone fits into a bowl-shaped socket in the hip-bone.

JOINT DESIGN

Joints come in many sizes and types. Each one determines how an animal moves. The orangutan is an ape, one of our closest cousins in the animal world. As it moves through the trees, its limbs reach out at almost any angle to grab the branches. Lift the see-through page to see each type of joint and how it works.

MUSCLE POWER

An animal cannot move using just bones and joints. It needs muscles! Muscles are like strings that can contract, or get shorter. Most muscles are attached to bones. As they contract, they pull the bones, and the animal moves. Watch how a baby mammal wobbles as it learns to walk. With more than 600 muscles in the body, it can have a tricky time!

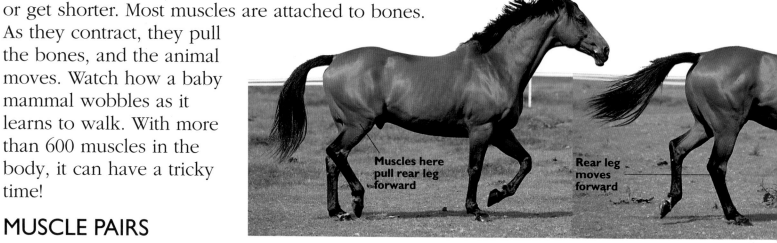

Muscles here pull rear leg forward

Rear leg moves forward

MUSCLE PAIRS

Although a muscle can *pull* very hard, it cannot get longer and *push*. Therefore many muscles work in pairs. One muscle pulls a bone one way. Its partner on the other side pulls the bone the other way. While one muscle shortens, the other relaxes and stretches.

The ends of a muscle are narrower and less fleshy than the middle, and they taper into rope-like tendons (see page 8). The ends of the tendons are anchored into the bones. As a weightlifter prepares for a lift, or a big cat prepares to pounce, you can often see the tendons rippling under the skin.

DID YOU KNOW?

In one test of its arm strength, a chimpanzee pulled the measuring meter four times harder than a grown man of the same weight.

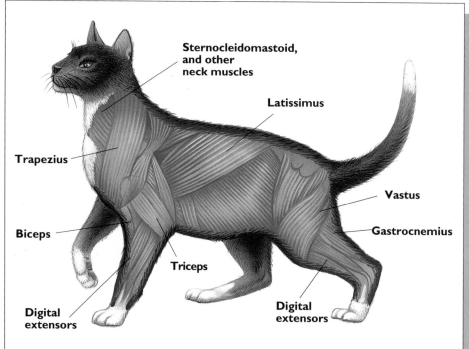

Sternocleidomastoid, and other neck muscles

Latissimus

Trapezius

Biceps

Triceps

Vastus

Gastrocnemius

Digital extensors

Digital extensors

In a typical mammal more than 600 muscles lie in layers, overlap, intertwine, and twist around each other to form a massive muscular network. Most of these muscle groups have long scientific names.

NEED FOR ENERGY

Muscles use up energy. The body eats and digests food to get energy-containing sugars, which are spread around the body in the blood. So a muscle contains lots of blood vessels.

Muscles also need oxygen. This comes from the air an animal breathes. An active animal's muscles need more oxygen, so it breathes faster and deeper.

For most movements, whole teams of muscles are contracting, relaxing, and continually making small adjustments. When a horse runs, the muscles on the front of each leg shorten to pull the leg forward (below left). Then the muscles behind the leg contract to pull it backward (below).

Muscles here pull rear leg backward

Mammal muscles come in different shapes and sizes, yet they are all much the same inside. A muscle is made of long strands called fibers. These are wrapped in groups, like bundles of string. When the muscle contracts, the fibers shorten and the muscle becomes almost half of its original length.

The gorilla's muscles are laid out in much the same way as your own. However, the gorilla has bigger neck, shoulder, and arm muscles in relation to its body size. A big male gorilla may have 155 pounds of muscle – the weight of an adult human.

Even on a hot, lazy day, this kangaroo uses muscles to make its ears twist and turn, listening for danger. Its eyes move using tiny muscles behind them. Muscles in its chest power its breathing.

ON THE WING

Bats are the only mammals to have mastered the art of flight. Their featherweight bodies are superbly designed for soaring and swooping, as they hunt insects and other small creatures. Only birds and some insects have also conquered the air. Of the 4,000 species of mammals, an amazing 1,000 are bats.

Thumb bones with claw

Wrist (carpals)

Forearm bone (radius)

Upper-arm bone (humerus)

Wing membrane (patagium)

Elbow

Large flight muscles in chest and shoulders

Ribs

Leg bones

Finger bone (of fourth finger)

Tail membrane (uropatagium)

Tailbones

FLAPPING FLIGHT

Over millions of years, the bat's arms and hands have evolved, or slowly changed, into wings. Instead of feathers, as on a bird, a bat's wings are covered with skin, called the wing membrane. The membrane is supported by long finger bones.

The bat's arms, shoulders, and chest have powerful muscles, which help flap the wings. The wings open on the downstroke, which gives a great push against the air. They partly fold on the upstroke, for less air resistance.

Bats, like this greater horseshoe bat, can catch insects such as moths and flies in mid-air. Some swoop down on mice and other creatures on the ground. A few snatch fish from the water with their hook-shaped foot claws. Others hover near flowers and sip the honey.

WINGS AND TAILS

The shapes of a bat's wings and tail show how it flies. The wing shapes are similar to bird wings, from gulls to hawks.

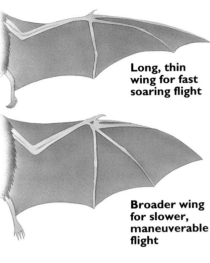

Long, thin wing for fast soaring flight

Broader wing for slower, maneuverable flight

Sheath-tailed bat, fast and maneuverable

Free-tailed bat, average flight

Short-tailed fruit bat, slow flight with long wingbeats

DID YOU KNOW?

◆ The smallest bat is Kitti's hog-nosed bat, from Southeast Asia. Its body is as small as your thumb.
◆ At one time, Europeans told stories about bats that sucked their victims' blood. The stories came true when explorers in South America discovered vampire bats, which really are bloodsuckers.
◆ The biggest bat is the greater flying fox. It's as big as a terrier dog, with wings 6 feet across.

GLIDERS

"Flying" squirrels and other "flying" mammals are really gliders. The flying squirrel has two folding flaps of furry skin along the sides of its body. It leaps from a branch, spreads its legs, and swoops downward on a skin-and-fur parachute. The squirrel steers by tilting its body and using its bushy tail.

The Southern flying squirrel usually leaps and glides when chased by a predator, such as a marten. It swoops down and lands low on a tree trunk, races up the trunk, and glides again. Big flying squirrels can cover more than 300 feet in one swoop.

Flying foxes (above) are large bats with doglike faces. They live in Asia, Africa, Australia, and the Pacific islands. Most of them glide by day, and they eat fruit, flowers, and other parts of plants.

SPLASHERS AND DIGGERS

If you have ever tried to run through a swimming pool, you know how difficult it is to move through water. Burrowing through soil is even slower and more difficult! Therefore, mammals that live in the water or under the ground have specially designed bodies for their way of moving.

DIGGING IN THE DIRT

Tunneling mammals, such as moles, usually have large claws, spade-shaped feet, and strong legs. The muscles in their shoulders are very powerful, too. The mole braces its rear feet against the tunnel wall as it works, scraping with its claws and pushing aside the soil with its snout, head, and shoulders. Some moles dig tunnels over 650 feet long!

A dolphin can swim upward so fast that it leaps clear of the water. Its most powerful muscles are along the top of its back. They shorten to pull the flukes, or tail fins, up. Other muscles along the belly pull the flukes down. Fish swim in a similar way to dolphins but their bodies arch from side to side.

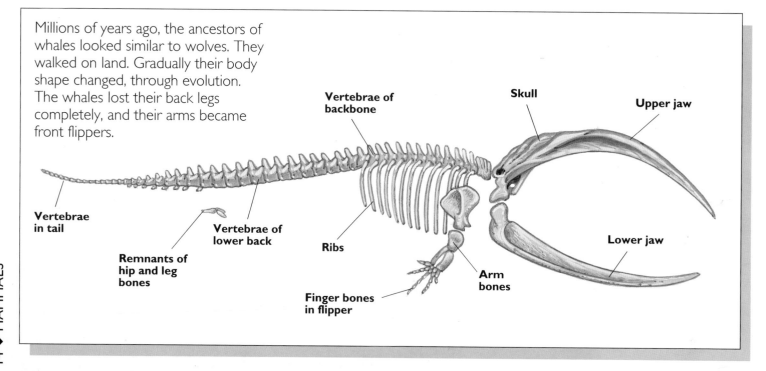

Millions of years ago, the ancestors of whales looked similar to wolves. They walked on land. Gradually their body shape changed, through evolution. The whales lost their back legs completely, and their arms became front flippers.

Vertebrae of backbone

Skull

Upper jaw

Vertebrae in tail

Remnants of hip and leg bones

Vertebrae of lower back

Ribs

Finger bones in flipper

Arm bones

Lower jaw

FLIPPERS...

Both seals and sea lions are streamlined for swimming in the ocean and can slide through the water with ease. However, they swim in different ways. Seals usually move by swishing the rear part of the body from side to side, and waving their rear flippers, which are really their legs. They hold their front flippers, or arms, against the body. Sea lions swim mainly by waving their front flippers like wings, as though rowing or "flying" through the water.

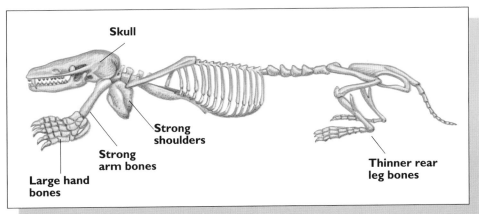

Skull

Strong shoulders

Strong arm bones

Large hand bones

Thinner rear leg bones

Compare this mole's skeleton with the skeletons of mammals shown on other pages. Its shoulder bones and front leg bones are very wide and strongly-built – ideal for digging.

The otter swims with its webbed feet. It spreads the toes and webs to get the greatest push backward against the water. As it pulls its feet forward, the toes come together, so there's less water resistance. Usually the hands are tucked into the body, but the otter sometimes paddles with them for extra speed.

...AND FLUKES

Dolphins and other whales have streamlined bodies, too. It seems as if their legs have turned into a two-part tail. But the tail, known as the flukes, is not the creature's legs. A dolphin has no real legs or leg bones. The flukes are mostly muscle. The dolphin swims by swishing the flukes up and down. Most of the power comes from the upstroke. The front flippers, which have hand bones inside, are used mainly for steering.

Like the mole, the Australian wombat is an expert digger and tunneler, as you can see from its strong, broad, spade-shaped hand (left). It digs rapidly to find food, to make a burrow, and to escape from enemies.

The mole shovels earth aside with its spade-shaped front feet. It feels its way through the dark underground tunnels using its sensitive nose and whiskers.

WALKING AND RUNNING

On land, too, mammal bodies have adapted to move in different ways. Some mammals, like the cheetah, are built for speed. Others, such as wolves and coyotes, are built for stamina, and can "dog-trot" for many miles as they follow their prey. A kangaroo bounces and leaps, and a sloth just hangs around all day!

The gibbon uses its long arms to swing through the trees. If the gibbon wants to move along a branch that is too thick to hold, it will run along the top on its back legs, holding its arms out for balance.

As a cheetah runs, it moves its long legs back and forth. It also bends its spine to arch its back up and then down, to gain even more speed. But, at full sprint, a cheetah cannot turn very fast. A prey that makes a sharp turn or swerves suddenly might get away.

ANIMAL SPRINTERS

Do you think you are a fast runner? Here are average sprint speeds for the racers and slowpokes on land. Many slow-looking creatures can run surprisingly fast to frighten enemies, or when they are in danger.

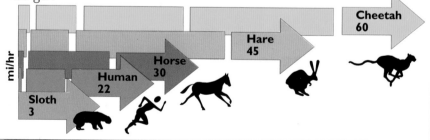

mi/hr

Sloth 3 | Human 22 | Horse 30 | Hare 45 | Cheetah 60

SPRINTERS

The cheetah is the fastest runner, capable of 60 miles an hour. It can sprint so fast because it has a very flexible skeleton. The hips and shoulders can swivel easily, so it has a long stride and can move its legs quickly.

LEAPERS AND SWINGERS

One of the most efficient ways of moving is by bouncing like a kangaroo. Powerful muscles in its big rear legs enable it to hop and spring across the ground. Some kangaroos can leap fences 10 feet high! Other mammals move by swinging through the trees, arm over arm. Mammals that do this usually have long, strong arms. The supreme tree-swinger is the gibbon of Southeast Asia. It can cover 30 feet in a single swing.

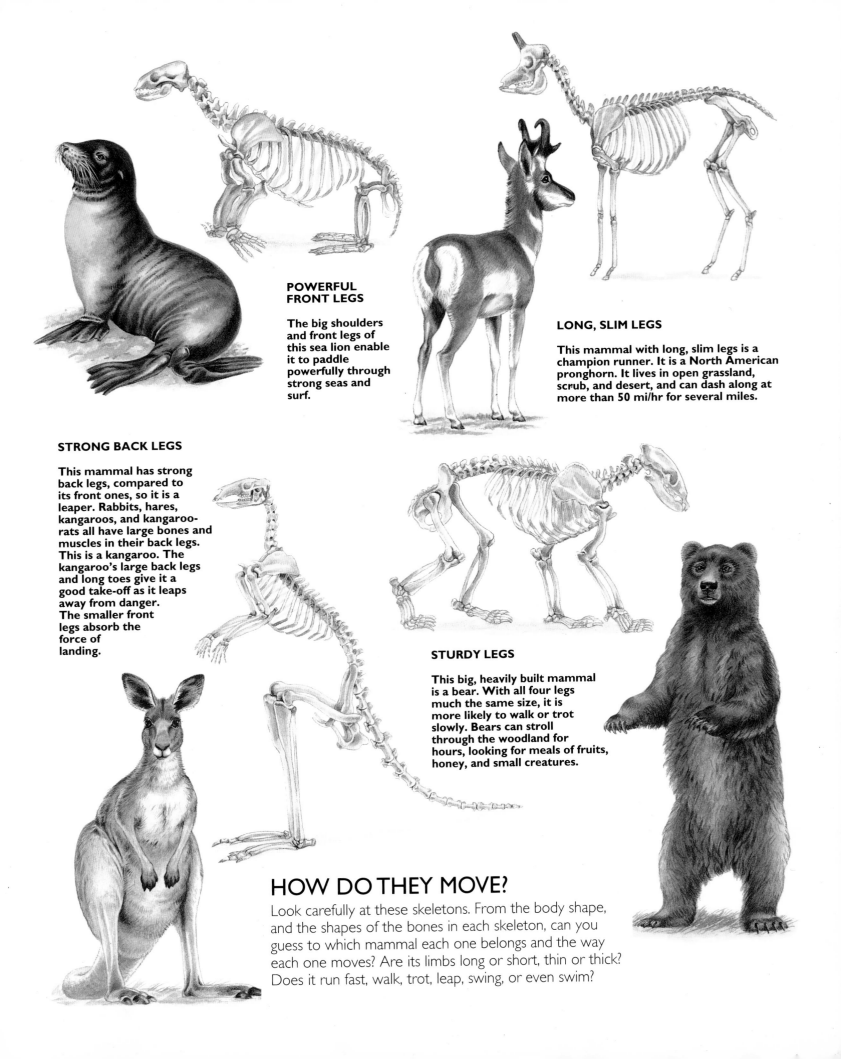

POWERFUL FRONT LEGS

The big shoulders and front legs of this sea lion enable it to paddle powerfully through strong seas and surf.

LONG, SLIM LEGS

This mammal with long, slim legs is a champion runner. It is a North American pronghorn. It lives in open grassland, scrub, and desert, and can dash along at more than 50 mi/hr for several miles.

STRONG BACK LEGS

This mammal has strong back legs, compared to its front ones, so it is a leaper. Rabbits, hares, kangaroos, and kangaroo-rats all have large bones and muscles in their back legs. This is a kangaroo. The kangaroo's large back legs and long toes give it a good take-off as it leaps away from danger. The smaller front legs absorb the force of landing.

STURDY LEGS

This big, heavily built mammal is a bear. With all four legs much the same size, it is more likely to walk or trot slowly. Bears can stroll through the woodland for hours, looking for meals of fruits, honey, and small creatures.

HOW DO THEY MOVE?

Look carefully at these skeletons. From the body shape, and the shapes of the bones in each skeleton, can you guess to which mammal each one belongs and the way each one moves? Are its limbs long or short, thin or thick? Does it run fast, walk, trot, leap, swing, or even swim?

A JIGSAW OF BONES

The skull is the main bone inside a mammal's head. Around or inside it are the nose, eyes, ears, jaws, teeth, and brain. In fact, the skull is made up of more than 20 bones, which fit like a curved jigsaw. Most of these bones grow and join firmly together during a mammal's early development.

ALL SHAPES AND SIZES

The skull provides vital support and protection for the main sense organs and the brain. Creatures which rely mostly on their sense of smell, such as dogs and horses, have a long-nosed skull.

A creature that depends chiefly on its sense of sight has very big eye sockets. The eyes of a bushbaby or kitten take up nearly half the head!

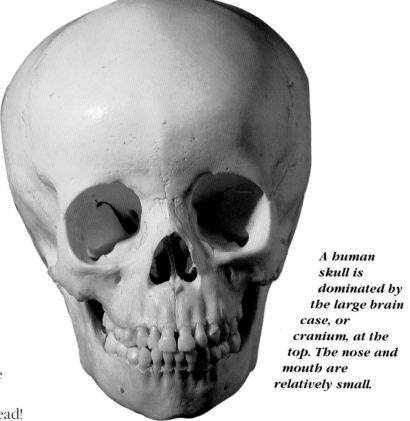

A human skull is dominated by the large brain case, or cranium, at the top. The nose and mouth are relatively small.

Frontal bone

Temporalis muscle

Upper jaw (maxilla)

Incisor teeth

Neck joint

Jaw joint

Canine teeth

Cheek bone (zygomatic arch)

Molar (carnassial, for cutting)

Lower jaw (mandible)

Masseter muscle

A lion is capable of killing its prey with one deadly bite. Four very strong muscles – two on either side of the head – raise the lower jaw toward the upper one, for biting.

PLANTS AND MEAT

The shape of the jaws and teeth show whether a mammal is an herbivore (plant eater), or a hunting carnivore (meat eater). Hunters have sharp teeth to grip their prey and tear it apart. In a big cat such as the lion, the longest teeth are the canine teeth, or fangs, near the front of the mouth. The lion uses them to spear and rip open its victim.

Most plant eaters have wide, flat-topped teeth for grinding and chewing grasses and leaves. Our own teeth are those of an omnivore ("anything eater"). We can eat most foods – meat, fruits, seeds, and plants.

THE JAW

The main movable bone in the skull is the mandible, or lower jaw. It is hinged to the skull at two joints, and teeth grow from both jawbones. Enamel, the teeth's whitish covering, is the hardest part of an animal's body.

Teeth are not simply lifeless hard lumps. The part above the gum is the crown. The part embedded in the jawbone is the root. Under the crown's hard enamel surface is a slightly less tough substance, dentine. In the tooth's center is the pulp cavity. This is filled with nerves and blood vessels, to feed the living tooth.

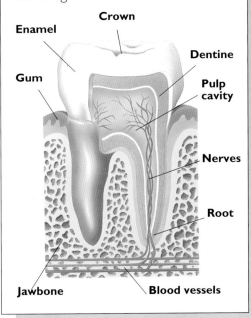

Crown
Enamel
Dentine
Gum
Pulp cavity
Nerves
Root
Jawbone
Blood vessels

The armadillo (above) has an extremely large snout, housing sensitive smelling parts in the nose and a long, strong tongue.

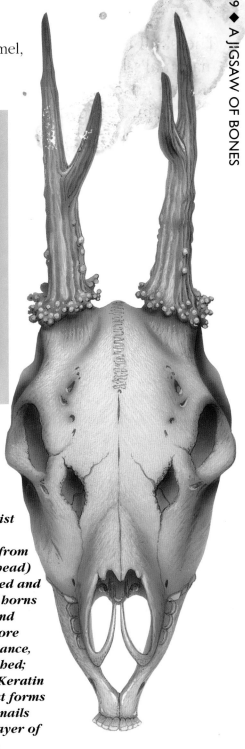

The antlers of deer consist of almost solid bone, as shown here. They grow from the skull's frontal (forehead) bone. The antlers are shed and regrown each year. The horns of cattle, sheep, goats, and antelopes have a bony core covered by a hard substance, keratin. Horns are not shed; they grow through life. Keratin is the same material that forms the hair and fur, claws, nails and hooves, and outer layer of the skin in all mammals.

The hippo's skull is shaped so that its eyes, ears, and nostrils are all at the top of its head. This means the hippo can lie almost submerged in the water with only the bumpy upper part of its head showing, and still see and breathe. It looks like an old, floating log.

INSIDE OUTSIDE

A rhino's skin is as thick as your thumb. A mouse's is thinner than this paper. A yak's skin sprouts hairs more than three feet long. And an armadillo has skin like hard plates of armor. Yet all of these body coverings are built from the same basic body parts. And their jobs are similar – to hold in body fluids, protect the body from knocks, bumps, and the sun's harmful rays, and keep these creatures warm and dry.

OUTER SKIN

Skin has two main layers. The outer one is the epidermis. Like other parts of the body, the epidermis is made of cells. On the skin's surface they are dead and flat, like tiles on a roof. Thousands are worn off the body every hour, by moving, rubbing, rain, and so on.

The lost cells are replaced by new ones that grow beneath them at the base of the epidermis. As they grow, these cells become hard and flat; they die as they are slowly pushed to the surface.

When you look at a mammal's skin, the bits you see are mostly dead. The outer skin and fur are not living. They are made of cells that have died and now form a strong, protective covering for the body.

Under a powerful microscope, a single hair resembles a thick piece of rope. It is entirely dead, made of flat cells joined together to form the rod shape of the hair.

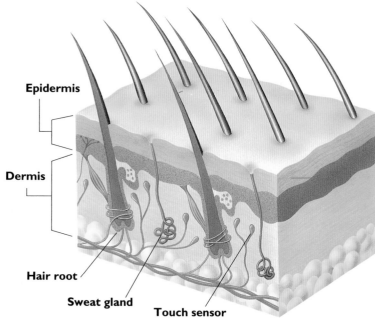

Epidermis

Dermis

Hair root

Sweat gland

Touch sensor

This is what a typical mammal's skin looks like under a microscope. The epidermis is on top, with its protective covering of hard, dead cells, which are filled with the tough protein keratin. The dermis below is alive with blood vessels, elastic fibers, and touch sensors.

INNER SKIN

Under the epidermis is the skin's second layer, the dermis. This mesh of tough, elastic fibers contains the microscopic sensors that detect touch, as well as tiny blood vessels and nerves.

Beneath the dermis is a layer of fat. In some animals, such as seals and whales and polar bears, this is many inches thick. It is called blubber, and it helps to keep their bodies warm in cold seas.

Whiskers are long hairs around the face. They help an animal to feel its way in the dark or in soil – or in water, if it's a walrus (right). The hairs themselves cannot feel anything because they are dead. Sensitive nerves wrapped around their roots detect the movements of the hairs as they rock and tilt.

The pangolin is known as the "animal pine cone." Its scales grow out of the skin, and are made of hard horn, similar to claws. They have a sharp, pointed edge. The pangolin can hang from branches with its prehensile (gripping) tail. When in danger, the pangolin curls into a sharp, scaly ball.

Fur helps to keep in the body's warmth. This Arctic hare has fluffed out its fur so that it is thicker, and traps more air. This makes an even better barrier against heat or cold. The Arctic hare's coat also provides camouflage (see page 40).

Broken skin and dirty fur can mean death for a mammal, because wounds get infected. Mammals, especially ones that live in water like the beaver below, clean their skin and comb their fur with their teeth and claws. Long, thick hairs form a tough guard coat for protection. Shorter hairs make a dense undercoat for warmth. Glands in the skin release natural oils to keep the skin and hairs supple (flexible) and waterproof.

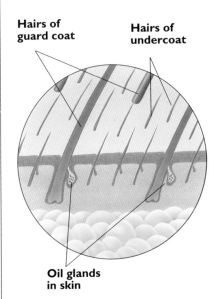

Hairs of guard coat

Hairs of undercoat

Oil glands in skin

On the porcupine, extra-large stiff hairs grow from the skin as spines. They give excellent prickly protection.

◆LUNGFULS OF AIR

Most mammals have to take air into their lungs every few seconds. Even those that live underwater, such as whales and seals, must come up for fresh air. This is because mammals need to take in new supplies of oxygen regularly to survive.

OXYGEN IN

Oxygen is all around us – it makes up one-fifth of the air. It is needed for chemical reactions that break down food. These reactions provide the body with energy and body-building materials.

The body's system for taking in oxygen is called the respiratory system. Its main parts are the nose, throat, windpipe (trachea), and lungs.

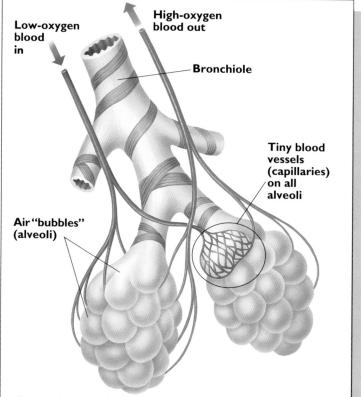

A lung is like a honeycomb. Small air tubes, called bronchioles, lead to air "bubbles," or alveoli. Wrapped around each alveoli is a web of tiny blood vessels. Blood turns from dark to bright red as it absorbs oxygen from the air in the alveoli.

Low-oxygen blood in

High-oxygen blood out

Bronchiole

Tiny blood vessels (capillaries) on all alveoli

Air "bubbles" (alveoli)

This is the respiratory system of a chamois. The lungs, along with the heart, fill the chest. They are protected by the bony bars of the ribs, which hinge up and down so the lungs can get bigger and smaller as the animal breathes.

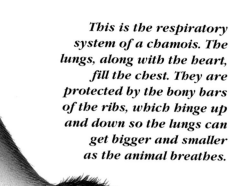

Nose

Throat

Windpipe (trachea)

Bronchus (main airway)

Lung

DID YOU KNOW?

At rest, you breathe in and out about 15 times a minute. This number rises to about 60 times a minute when you are active and panting to take in more air. Bigger mammals breathe slower. A resting elephant takes about 6 breaths each minute. A mouse takes about 250!

DEEP IN THE LUNGS

When a mammal breathes in, it sucks oxygen-rich air down its throat. The air flows along a strong tube in its neck called the windpipe. This can twist and turn as the mammal moves its head, while remaining open for breathing.

The windpipe divides into two air tubes, called bronchi, that lead to the two lungs in the chest. The bronchi divide again and again, becoming as narrow as one of your hairs. The smallest tubes end in bunches of microscopic bubbles, called alveoli, which are surrounded by a network of tiny blood vessels. Oxygen from the air seeps through the linings of the bubbles, into the blood, and is carried off around the body.

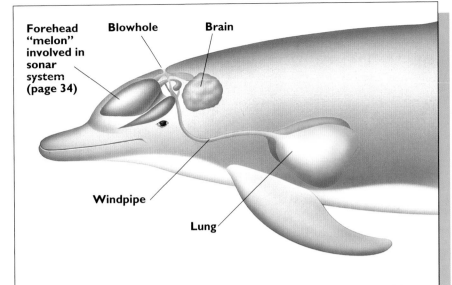

Forehead "melon" involved in sonar system (page 34) **Blowhole** **Brain**

Windpipe

Lung

Whales and dolphins have nostrils on the tops of their heads! The two nostrils on this dolphin are joined to make a single opening called the blowhole. The dolphin breathes in deeply, then closes the blowhole with a flap of muscular skin as it dives. This skin prevents water from leaking in.

POISONS OUT

The lungs also get rid of carbon dioxide, which is made during the body's chemical reactions. If carbon dioxide builds up in the blood, it is poisonous. So it seeps from the blood into the air in the lungs, and is blown away as the mammal breathes out.

There are over 300 million alveoli in each lung. They give a huge surface area for absorbing oxygen. Spread out, the alveoli in a human's lungs would cover a tennis court.

Like many mammals, a wolf uses breathed-out air to make noise. In the voice box, two flaps of skin, called vocal cords, move over the windpipe. The air rushes past the vocal cords, which vibrate and make sounds.

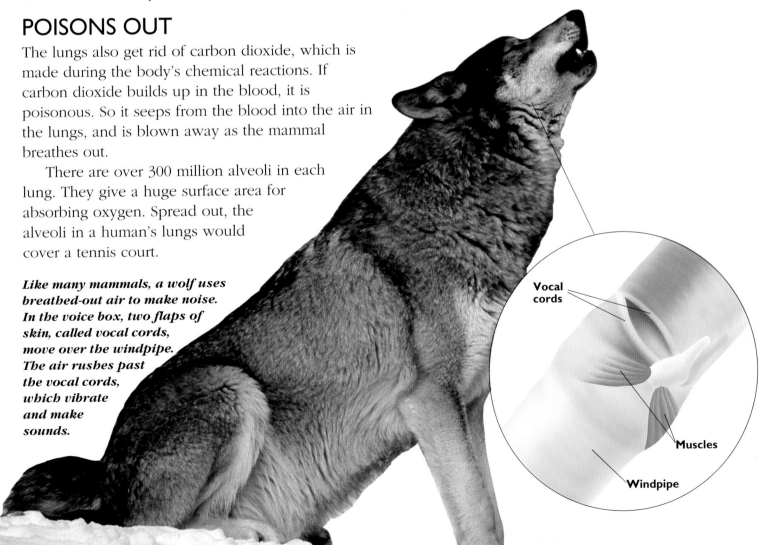

Vocal cords

Muscles

Windpipe

THE BEATING HEART

Inside every mammal, in the center of its chest, lies a beating heart. In all of them the heart is remarkably similar. Only the size varies, to fit the body.

TWO PUMPS IN ONE

The heart is a hollow muscular bag divided into two parts, a left pump and a right pump. The left pump sends blood around the whole body. The blood supplies the body with warmth, oxygen, and vital nutrients for energy, growth, and repair.

The blood then goes to the other side of the heart, the right pump. This pump sends it on a much shorter journey to the lungs, where the blood picks up fresh supplies of oxygen. From there it flows around to the left pump, ready to start all over again.

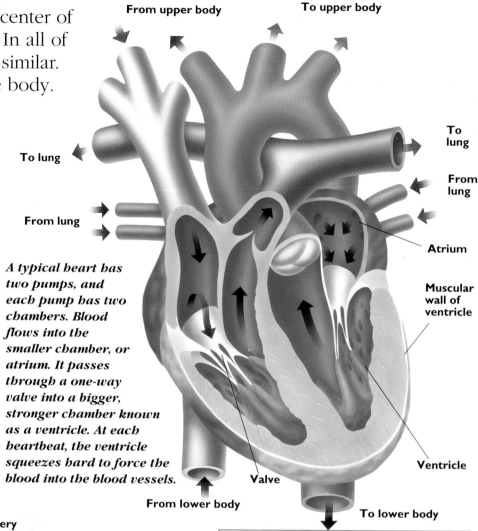

From upper body

To upper body

To lung

From lung

To lung

From lung

Atrium

Muscular wall of ventricle

Ventricle

Valve

From lower body

To lower body

A typical heart has two pumps, and each pump has two chambers. Blood flows into the smaller chamber, or atrium. It passes through a one-way valve into a bigger, stronger chamber known as a ventricle. At each heartbeat, the ventricle squeezes hard to force the blood into the blood vessels.

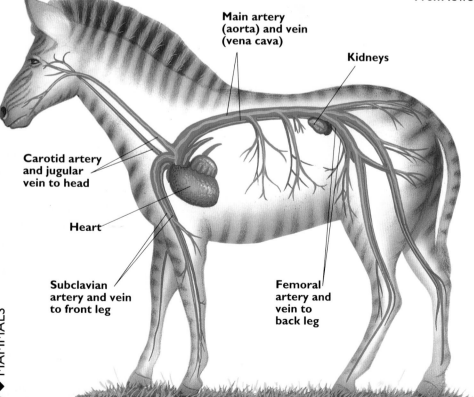

Main artery (aorta) and vein (vena cava)

Kidneys

Carotid artery and jugular vein to head

Heart

Subclavian artery and vein to front leg

Femoral artery and vein to back leg

HEART RATES

(Average rates at rest, in beats per minute)

Blue whale 6   Elephant 25   Horse 28

Human 78   Dog 140   Shrew 900

Measure your own heart rate by feeling for the pulse in your wrist, below your thumb. Each pulse is one heartbeat.

Blood vessels spread out from the heart and reach all parts of the body (left), even the toes. Red blood cells carry oxygen along the arteries. Blood that has delivered its oxygen comes back to the heart along veins.

Your heart is as big as your clenched fist. A shrew's heart is little bigger than a baked bean. A blue whale's heart is almost as big as a small car. In relation to the whole body, though, it is much the same size in all mammals.

Another thing blood does is collect waste chemicals from the body. It takes them to the kidneys, which filter them into a fluid called urine. This rhinoceros is expelling its plentiful urine.

BLOOD TUBES

Blood flows to the body through strong blood vessels, known as arteries. Arteries divide many times, getting smaller and smaller. They become a network of tiny blood vessels thinner than hairs, called capillaries. The capillaries reach into every bit of the body. They join again to form larger blood vessels, the veins, which take blood back to the heart.

DID YOU KNOW?
◆ The adult human body contains about 7-10 pints of blood.
◆ A big whale has 20,000 pints of blood, enough to fill 100 bathtubs!

In order to survive very cold winter weather, some mammals hibernate. Like this dormouse, they go into a sleep-like state for many weeks, with their body temperatures and pulses and breathing rates lowered. A hibernating dormouse breathes only once every five minutes.

WARM BLOOD

Mammals are "warm-blooded" – they use their blood to maintain a constant body temperature. When the body is too hot, the blood carries heat out to the skin. In the cold, the blood takes short-cuts through blood vessels that are not so close to the skin, so that less heat is lost from the body.

Blood is a symbol of life – and death. Hunters tend to "go for the throat," where there are many large blood vessels. A big cat like this cheetah attacks by slashing with its claws and biting with its teeth. It tears open an animal's throat and neck, and the victim bleeds to death. Then the cheetah can enjoy its meal.

If bacteria or viruses get into the body, white cells in the blood produce antibodies, chemicals that attack invaders. Here a white blood cell is about to engulf a bacteria (bottom) that causes sore throats.

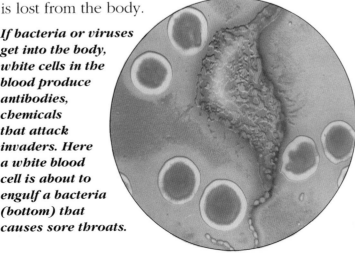

FEEDING TIME

Every mammal needs to eat and drink to survive. Food provides the energy for it to live and move, and the nutrients it needs to grow and repair itself. In the wild, animals take every opportunity to eat as much as they can. An Asian wild dog can gobble as much food at one meal as you eat in four days! For it might not find any food at all next week.

Gullet (esophagus)

Throat (pharynx)

FIRST STOP FOR FOOD

Once the food is found, it must be swallowed and digested, to get nourishment into the body. First, the swallowed food goes into the stomach. This is a muscular bag that can stretch to hold a large meal. The stomach squirms and squeezes and squashes the food, and mixes it with strong chemicals to make a thick soup.

GETTING THE GOODNESS

Next, the food soup passes into the intestines. Here nutrients pass from the digested food into the blood system, to be taken around the body. The body also stores some nutrients as fat, for use when there's a shortage of food. The leftovers, or wastes, are stored at the end of the intestines. The animal gets rid of them as droppings.

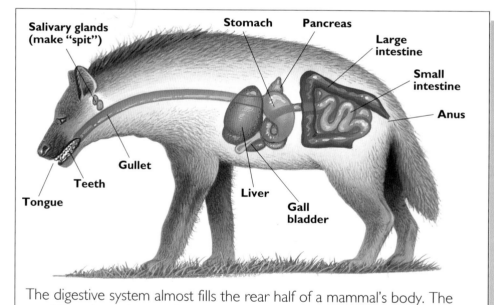

Salivary glands (make "spit") · Stomach · Pancreas · Large intestine · Small intestine · Anus · Gullet · Teeth · Tongue · Liver · Gall bladder

The digestive system almost fills the rear half of a mammal's body. The small intestine is long and thin, and absorbs most of the nourishment. The large intestine is short and wide, and absorbs water from the leftovers.

A lion rests for much of its life. On average, it eats only one-fortieth of its own weight each day, because its meaty meal is so nourishing. There is usually one big feed every few days, with long rests between.

THE LIVER

The liver plays an important role. It makes some of the chemicals that digest the food, ensures the body gets the right amounts of nutrients, and stores energy until it is needed. It also cleans the blood and prepares waste chemicals for disposal by the kidneys.

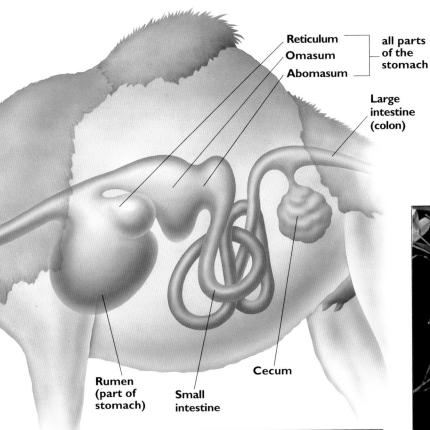

Reticulum
Omasum
Abomasum
} all parts of the stomach

Large intestine (colon)

Cecum

Rumen (part of stomach)

Small intestine

Some plant eaters (such as the camel, left) have extra-large stomachs with several chambers. They are called "ruminants." They swallow food into the rumen, where it begins to digest. Later they bring up the softened food and chew it, to extract more nutrients. Then they swallow the food again. It passes to the other stomach chambers, and on to the intestine in the usual way. Deer, antelope, cattle, camels, and giraffes are all ruminants.

Plant foods usually have fewer nutrients than meat. So plant eaters need to eat more than meat eaters, and that takes longer. An elephant (above) takes in one-twentieth of its body weight daily as food. That means eating 330 pounds of grass, leaves, twigs, fruit, and roots – the same weight as two or three people!

Scientists group China's panda with the carnivores – the meat-eating mammals. Yet it hardly ever eats meat, only bamboo shoots, stems, and leaves.

The giant anteater lives in South America. It doesn't have any teeth, but it can poke out its tongue more than 20 inches. When it finds an ants' nest, the anteater flicks out its tongue twice a second. More than 20 ants stick to it each time.

ON THE SCENT

Humans rely greatly on sight. More than two-thirds of our attention is taken up by what we see. So it is difficult to appreciate that other mammals rely much more on their other senses. Smell, hearing, touch, and taste help them in the daily struggle to find food and avoid predators and other dangers.

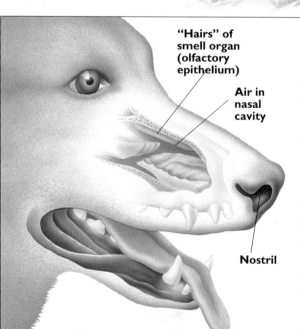

Dogs such as bloodhounds have been specially bred for their ability to follow scents, especially of humans. A microscopic trail of skin and hair fragments shower down around a walking person – more than 1,000 bits every second. The dog can follow that trail by its smell.

"Hairs" of smell organ (olfactory epithelium)

Air in nasal cavity

Nostril

A dog's hairy smell organ covers the wavy skull bone in the roof of its nasal cavity. With an area of 23 square inches, it is more than 30 times larger than our own smell organ. A bloodhound can pick up smells thousands of times weaker than those we can detect.

THE WORLD IN SMELLS

Many mammals get a lot of information from their noses. Air passes into their bodies every few seconds as they breathe. So it makes sense to check this air for important smells. While they feed, creatures such as rabbits and antelopes pause now and then, and stretch up to sniff the air. They are smelling for predators (enemies), for members of their own herd or group, for rivals from other groups, and even for the scent of approaching rain or fire.

Awful odors are a good way of getting rid of enemies! The skunk is famous for the foul-smelling fluid that it can squirt from under its tail. It stinks up everything it lands on.

INSIDE THE NOSE

Inside a mammal's nose is an air-filled chamber, the nasal cavity. In the chamber's roof is a patch of hair-like endings that resembles a worn-out toothbrush. This is part of the olfactory, or smell, organ. As air flows through the chamber, tiny particles settle onto the "hairs." Some trigger nerve signals (see page 30) that flash to the mammal's brain, so that it is aware of the smell.

Many creatures use smells as messages, saying "I own this patch of land!" Antelope smear a smelly fluid, from glands below their eyes, onto trees in their area. Antelope from other herds smell the fluid and know the territory is occupied.

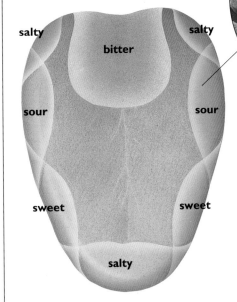

Different parts of the tongue detect different flavors. The many flavors we taste are made from combinations of four basic ones: sweet, salty, sour, and bitter.

salty · bitter · salty · sour · sour · sweet · sweet · salty

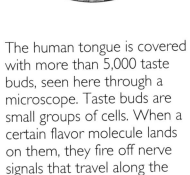

The human tongue is covered with more than 5,000 taste buds, seen here through a microscope. Taste buds are small groups of cells. When a certain flavor molecule lands on them, they fire off nerve signals that travel along the nerves to the brain.

TESTING FOOD

When feeding, mammals will sniff the meal cautiously, and then give it a couple of licks to get the initial flavors. If the food smells or tastes unfamiliar or bad, the mammal might ignore the meal.

Even dirty, rotten bits of animals and plants may contain nourishment. Raccoons use their senses of smell and taste to avoid natural poisons. It might not be delicious, but it is better than starving.

UNDER CONTROL

A mammal's senses work by changing what it detects into tiny electric signals, called nerve signals. Eyes detect light rays and turn them into nerve signals. Ears do the same with sound waves. Noses detect airborne odors; tongues detect flavors; and skin detects touch and movement.

A NETWORK OF NERVES

The signals created by all these sensations pass along nerves inside the animal's body. The entire nervous system is built of microscopic nerve cells. Each has threadlike "fingers" that connect to other nerve cells. The cells are bundled together in the thousands to make small nerves, thick as a piece of wire. Millions of nerve cells make up the rope-sized main nerves. The brain is made up of billions of these nerve cells.

NERVE SIGNALS

The fastest nerve signals travel at many feet per second. In a small mammal like a gerbil, they go from the skin on the tip of its tail to its brain in less than one-tenth of a second.

The life of this gerbil depends on its nerves and quick reactions. If it hears a strange noise, its ears send nerve signals into its brain. The brain sends signals out to its leg muscles. In a split second, the gerbil has leaped to safety.

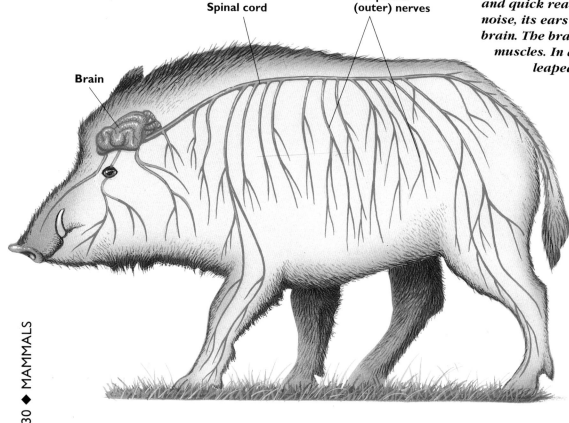

Brain

Spinal cord

Peripheral (outer) nerves

This is the nervous system of a typical mammal, the wild boar. The brain sits inside the skull bone of the head. A thick bundle of nerves called the spinal cord extends from the brain down through the row of backbones, called the spine. The brain and spinal cord make up the central nervous system. Smaller nerves branch from the brain and spinal cord, all over the body. These nerves make up the peripheral nervous system.

SIGNALS IN

There are three main types of nerves. Sensory nerves carry signals from the sense organs, such as the eyes and ears, to the brain. The second type of nerves, intermediate or relay nerves, pass nerve signals from one nerve cell to another, especially in the brain.

SIGNALS OUT

The third type of nerve carries nerve signals from the brain to the muscles. These are motor nerves. When the signals reach a muscle, they tell it to contract, or shorten. As nerve signals flash from the brain to dozens of muscles, at precisely the right time, a mammal makes smooth, coordinated movements. Nerve signals also help to control the muscles in the heart, the chest, the intestines, and other internal organs.

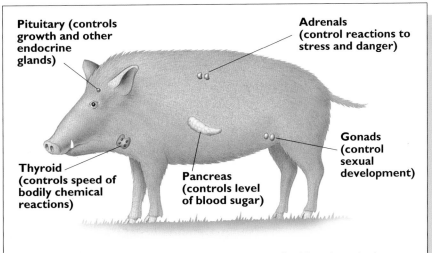

The mongoose is famed for its lightning reactions. It can even dodge the bite of a striking cobra, and then dart in to deliver a killing bite to the snake's neck.

Pituitary (controls growth and other endocrine glands)

Adrenals (control reactions to stress and danger)

Thyroid (controls speed of bodily chemical reactions)

Pancreas (controls level of blood sugar)

Gonads (control sexual development)

Some long-term body functions are controlled by chemicals called hormones that circulate in the blood. Hormones are made in endocrine glands (above). Some diseases are the result of too much or too little of a particular hormone being released.

In top-class tennis, players can serve a ball at over 100 miles an hour. The other player has less than a second from when the ball leaves the racquet, to move into position and make the return stroke.

INSIDE THE BRAIN

A mammal's brain looks like a lump of grayish pink jelly. But it is really an amazing network of billions of nerve cells. These cells process signals arriving from the outer nerves, and allow the animal to perform hundreds of activities.

PARTS OF THE BRAIN

The brain has several main parts. The brain stem controls body processes such as the heartbeat and breathing. These are activities that happen automatically. The lowest part of the brain stem is the medulla, which narrows and joins the spinal cord.

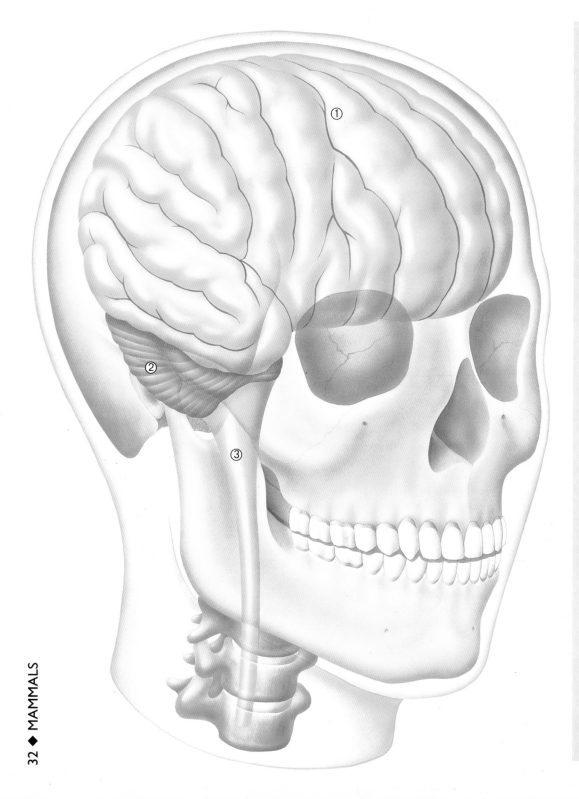

THE BRAIN

A human's brain (left) fits in the top part of the bony skull, the cranium. It is surrounded by fluid that helps nourish the brain and collects wastes. The brains of a cat, rabbit, monkey, and elephant are shown on the right.

I The cerebrum is the main part of the brain. It forms nine-tenths of the brain's volume. It is divided into two halves called cerebral hemispheres.
2 The cerebellum co-ordinates our muscles to make complex movements.
3 The spinal cord is a long, large nerve that connects the brain to the rest of the body.

Certain areas of the brain (far right) receive, process, and interpret nerve signals from our senses.
I The visual center receives nerve signals from our eyes.
2 The hearing center receives signals from our ears.
3 The smell center receives nerve signals from our nose.
4 The touch center receives nerve signals from our skin.
5 The speech center controls our voice box and speech.
6 The pre-frontal lobes deal with second-by-second input from our senses, giving us continuously updated awareness of objects around us.
7 The motor center begins and controls basic movement.

Now turn the see-through page to see...

CHAMBERS AND LOBES

At the rear of the brain is the cerebellum, made up of two wrinkled lobes. They help to control the body's muscles, making sure that complicated movements are carried out smoothly.

At the base of the cerebrum is the hypothalamus. This small area deals with basic needs such as hunger, thirst, and the urge to breed.

The cerebrum is the largest part of the mammal brain. It is the top part of the brain and consists of two dome-shaped wrinkled lobes known as the cerebral hemispheres.

THINKING

The cerebral hemispheres analyze nerve signals coming in from the senses and send out nerve signals to the muscles. And the many mental activities we call "thinking" – such as remembering things, reasoning, and making choices and decisions – occur in this part of the brain.

INSIDE THE BRAIN

The face and brain receive oxygen, nourishment, and warmth from the blood flowing through arteries and veins (left). A network of nerves (below left) surrounds the face, too.

The diagram opposite shows:
1 The cerebral cortex, or "gray matter," involved with senses, initiating movements, thinking, and memory.
2 "White matter," consisting mainly of nerve fibers.
3 The corpus callosum, which links the cerebral hemispheres.
4 The thalamus, which relays signals going to different parts of the brain.
5 The limbic system, involved with our emotions, such as sorrow, fear, and guilt.
6 The tectum, involved in thinking and memory.
7 The hypothalamus, which deals with basic feelings.
8 The medulla, which controls life processes such as heartbeat and breathing.

The diagram on the right shows how nerve signals from each eye divide at the optic chiasma, so that each of the brain's visual centers receives signals from both eyes.
1 The optic nerves.
2 The optic chiasma.
3 The lateral geniculate bodies are relay stations.
4 The left and right visual centers.

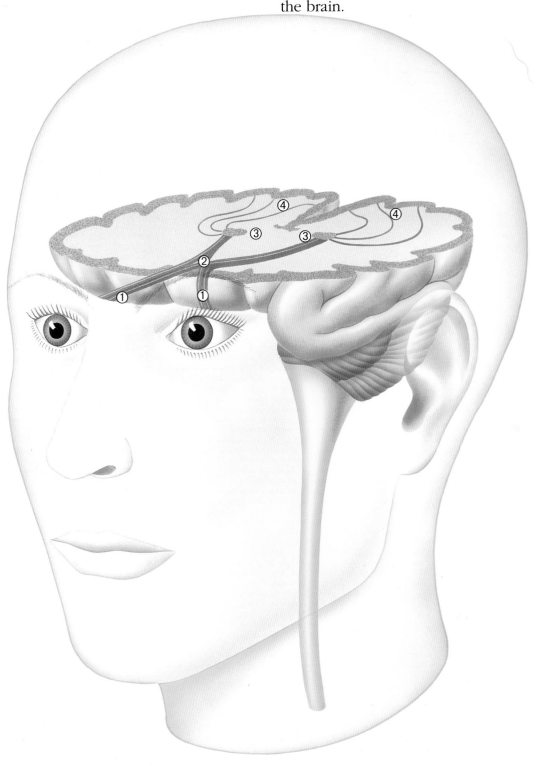

RATTLE AND ROLL

Ears tell a mammal a great deal about the world. Few predators can move in complete silence, so a rustled leaf or cracked twig warns of approaching danger. Ears also hear messages – the grunt of elephants, the bellow of seals, the whoops of monkeys, and the chatter of humans.

EAR FLAPS

Ears are designed to detect sound waves. Sound waves are invisible vibrations of molecules in the air that pass outward from whatever is making the sound.

The outer ear is the part on the side of the head. Rabbits, horses, giraffes, and many other mammals have large outer ears, for collecting as many sound waves as possible. These large ear flaps make their hearing more sensitive. Seals have two tiny ear holes, since big ear flaps would slow them down when swimming.

INSIDE THE EAR

Mammals' ears all work in the same way. The ear flap leads into a short tunnel inside the head. At the end of this tunnel, which is about one inch long in humans, is the eardrum. The eardrum is a tiny piece of skin, as big as a little fingernail, stretched tight. It vibrates, or shakes slightly, as sound waves hit it.

A typical bat can fly through darkness in complete safety. The bat makes quick squeaks, too high-pitched for most people to hear. The bat listens to the returning echoes with its large radar-dish ears. From the echo pattern it can figure out the distances and shapes of objects, such as a likely moth meal. This system is called "echolocation."

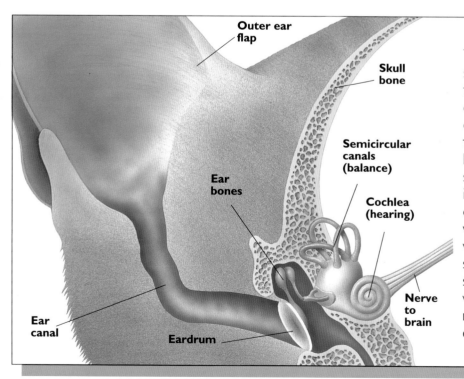

Outer ear flap

Skull bone

Semicircular canals (balance)

Ear bones

Cochlea (hearing)

Nerve to brain

Ear canal

Eardrum

The outer ear is a sound-gathering funnel. The middle ear consists of the eardrum and three tiny bones in a hole inside the skull bone. The inner ear consists of the cochlea, which changes vibrations to nerve signals, and three semicircular canals, which give a mammal its sense of balance.

Dolphins, like bats, find their way and their prey using their hearing! They utter high clicks and squeaks. The dolphins can figure out the shape and distance of each object from the pattern of echoes.

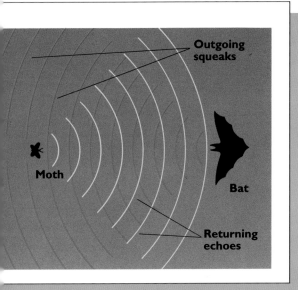

Outgoing squeaks

Moth

Bat

Returning echoes

RATTLING BONES

The back-and-forth shakes and rattles of the vibrations in the eardrum pass along to three tiny bones. These are known as the hammer, anvil, and stirrup, because of their shapes. They are the smallest bones in a mammal's body.

Finally, the vibrations pass into a pale yellow liquid inside the cochlea. The cochlea changes the vibrations into nerve signals, which travel to the brain to be analyzed.

This harvest mouse can climb into many awkward positions, yet keep its balance even in high wind. Inside a mammal's ear is a liquid that moves as its body moves. The moving liquid touches special hairs. Nerves connected to the hairs tell the brain what position the body is in, so helping the mammal keep its balance.

The big ears of the fennec fox are ideal for listening for the scratchy sounds of tiny prey like beetles and lizards. Also, the ears work like heat radiators. They help the fox to get rid of excess body warmth, so that it does not overheat in the desert sun. An elephant's ears are huge for the same reason.

SOUNDS

Some mammals can hear sounds that are too low or too high for us to detect. Usually this is because they make sounds at that pitch, too.

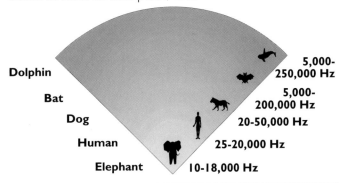

Dolphin	5,000-250,000 Hz
Bat	5,000-200,000 Hz
Dog	20-50,000 Hz
Human	25-20,000 Hz
Elephant	10-18,000 Hz

Can you wiggle your ears? Mammals such as hares, rabbits, horses, and deer can. It helps them to find the direction of a sound without looking around.

THE WORKING EYE

The eye is incredibly complex and delicate. It detects shapes, colors, and movements, alters itself to see near and distant objects, and adjusts for bright and dim light. In all mammals this happens in a globe of jelly about an inch across.

LIKE A CAMERA

The eye is a little like a camera. For example, the camera has a hole at the front, to let light into the interior. So does the eye. It is called the pupil, and it's surrounded by a ring of muscles called the iris. The iris makes the pupil smaller in bright light, to protect the delicate interior. In dim conditions it opens wide to let in as much light as possible.

Each eyeball is protected at the sides and back by a bowl-shaped piece of skull bone known as the orbit, or eye socket. It is moved by six tiny muscles around it, so the mammal can swivel its eyes up and down, and from side to side.

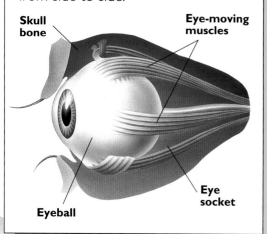

Skull bone

Eye-moving muscles

Eyeball

Eye socket

Sclera is eyeball's strong outer coat

Eyelid closes to protect eyes

Iris controls size of pupil

Pupil lets light rays into eye

Lens focuses light rays onto retina

Tear duct

Optic nerve sends nerve signals to brain

Retina turns light rays into nerve signals

Choroid contains blood vessels to nourish eye

Transparent jelly keeps eye's ball shape

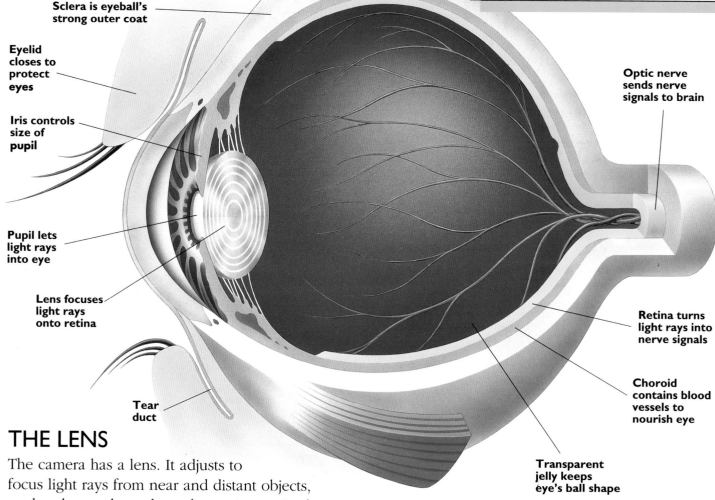

THE LENS

The camera has a lens. It adjusts to focus light rays from near and distant objects, so that they make a clear, sharp picture. So does the eye, but the lens works in a different way. The camera's lens moves back and forward. The eye's lens adjusts the focus by changing its shape, from thin to fat.

Dim light

Bright light

The pupil is the "window" at the front of the eye that lets light inside. Our eyes have round pupils. Some mammals, such as cats, have slit-shaped pupils, which give them a squinty-eyed appearance.

THE RETINA

A camera has film, a thin layer that detects light rays. So does the eye. This layer is called the retina. It contains millions of tiny cells. Each cell contains chemicals that change when light rays hit them. As the chemical changes, it fires off a nerve signal that flashes to the brain. Millions of chemical changes take place every second to make a picture of what you are reading.

This is the eye's retina, magnified many thousands of times. The long green cylinders are rod cells, which detect light and dark. The shorter orange objects in the lower center are cone cells, which pick up colors. You have 120 million rods and seven million cones in each eye!

Outline (Form)

Movement (Motion)

Color

Shape (Depth)

When we look at an object, we "see" it in several ways – its outline, how it moves, its color, and its overall shape. This information is sorted by the brain to give us a picture of the object.

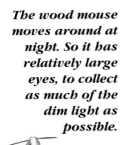

The wood mouse moves around at night. So it has relatively large eyes, to collect as much of the dim light as possible.

Most mammals can see some colors, but probably not the same ones as we can. A squirrel monkey at a zoo might have this limited color view of people looking at it. Dogs probably see colors as various shades of gray.

EYES FOR SEEING

You can probably guess whether a mammal hunts or is hunted by looking at its eyes. Predators usually have two forward-facing eyes at the front of the head. Hunted creatures generally have eyes on the sides of the head. Can you figure out why they are different?

AN ALL-AROUND VIEW

The arrangement of a mammal's eyes depends on how much of its surroundings the mammal needs to see. This is linked to its way of life.

Mammals such as rabbits, antelopes, and horses are the prey of hunters. Therefore they have eyes that are relatively large, and stick out from the side of the head so that the mammal can see in front, to the side, and even behind. This is very useful when keeping a look out for predators sneaking up from behind.

In the African bush, meerkats stand on their hind legs to look about. Their main enemies are birds of prey. Meerkats have superb eyesight to see birds while they are still distant spots in the sky.

EYES TO THE FRONT

The eyes of predators such as tigers, weasels, and seals are closer together, at the front of the head. Both eyes point forward.

This arrangement may seem a disadvantage because the predator can only see in front of it, unless it turns its head. However, a fierce hunter doesn't really need to worry about things creeping up on it. The advantages are much greater than the disadvantages. Because the view from their eyes overlaps in the middle, mammals can see details much more clearly.

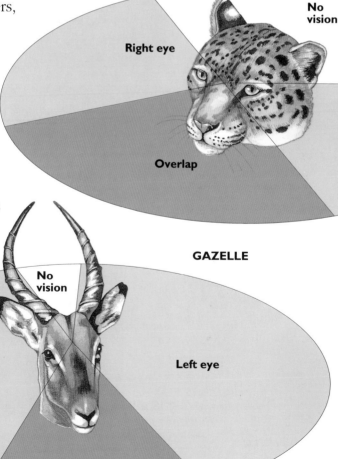

LEOPARD

No vision

Right eye

Left eye

Overlap

GAZELLE

No vision

Right eye

Left eye

Overlap

The leopard's eyes only see a front view, but in greater detail, and with the ability to judge distances precisely. It does not need to watch for predators. The gazelle has wide-set eyes, which are able to see in front and behind at the same time. This helps it to keep watch for hunters such as the leopard.

JUDGING DISTANCES

The overlap also helps a predator to judge distances. This is because each eye sees things from a slightly different angle. You can find this out yourself. Look at a nearby object, first with only one eye, then with only the other. See how the view changes slightly.

The predator's brain compares the different view from each eye and is able to figure out accurately how far away its prey is – and how far it has to chase or pounce on the victim.

The naked mole rat lives its entire life underground, in the African grasslands. It is so dark in the burrows that this rodent's tiny eyes are covered by skin. It can hardly see anything.

When we look at objects, we use light and shade to help figure out their shape. We assume that the light comes from one direction, such as the sun. Can you see the cross of bumps on the pattern below? Now turn it upside down. It has become a cross of dips! This is because your brain thinks that the lighter and shaded areas on the drawing are caused by a single source of light, usually from above.

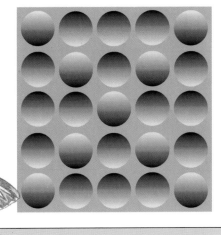

The African bushbaby feeds at night on small creatures and plants. It has huge eyes to gather what little light there is. Like some other mammals that are active at night, such as cats, its eyes are designed to direct as much light as possible onto the retina. When hunting, the bushbaby waits on a branch. Then, using its eyes and sensitive hearing, the bushbaby reaches out and grabs its prey.

COLORS AND CAMOUFLAGE

Many mammals have colors and patterns that blend in with their surroundings. This camouflage helps hide them from predators, which uses less energy than running from danger. Browns, especially, merge with old leaves and grass, making an animal hard to spot.

Tiny grains of melanin are made by tiny cells in the skin. The grains settle between and within other skin cells, and in hairs as they grow.

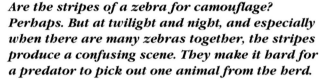

Hair

Melanocyte

Melanin granules

Are the stripes of a zebra for camouflage? Perhaps. But at twilight and night, and especially when there are many zebras together, the stripes produce a confusing scene. They make it hard for a predator to pick out one animal from the herd.

A CONCEALING CHEMICAL

The skin and fur colors of mammals, from pink and red to brown and black, are due to a chemical called melanin. Each color is made by different amounts and patterns of melanin, and whether the flesh and blood show through. A polar bear's fur is white because it has no melanin at all. A black bear's fur contains lots of melanin.

CHANGING COATS

In summer, the brown fur of the Arctic hare provides camouflage among leaves and dry grass. In autumn, its fur gradually falls out, and white fur grows in its place. In the snow of the cold North, this fur hides the hare from predators. But one of the hare's enemies, the Arctic fox, has white fur in winter, too. It can approach its prey unseen.

The black panther is not a separate species of big cat, like the tiger, lion, cheetah, jaguar, or leopard. It is an almost black form of the leopard. Black panthers are born only rarely, to typically colored, spotted leopard parents.

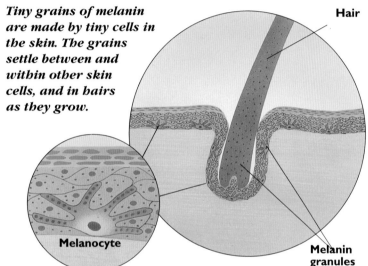

Even the sharp-eyed jaguar has difficulty spotting the motionless and camouflaged three-toed sloth. The sloth's long hair is a subtle mixture of many colors. It is also grooved, and tiny plants called algae grow in it! The sloth's amazing natural camouflage makes it look just like drooping lichen or a hanging ant's nest.

The ocelot, a small cat, hunts at night and is an agile climber. Its spots and stripes are difficult to see in the moonlight filtering through the trees.

The palm squirrel's brown fur is a close match to the bark of the swamp palm, its favorite tree. This squirrel presses itself against the trunk and stays completely still, and becomes invisible.

The chital, or spotted axis deer, dwells in the forests of India and Sri Lanka. The white spots on its back and sides mimic small patches of bright sunlight shining through the trees.

CAMOUFLAGE

Fur colors and patterns may disguise a mammal. Or they may break up its outline, so that its body shape is less obvious. Pandas and badgers have this type of coloring. In the wild, among the striped grasses and shadowy trees, it is an excellent form of camouflage. Can you spot the several types of camouflage shown in the picture before lifting up the see-through page?

◆BREEDING TIME

The previous pages have looked at different features of mammals' bodies, all essential for survival. There is one more important set of parts – vital not just for survival, but for life itself. These are the reproductive organs, for making baby mammals that will continue the species.

PICKING PARTNERS

Many mammals go through a period of courtship before they mate with a partner. A male walrus, for example, sings "love songs" to a female. These include noises like bells, claps, and whistles.

Courtship has several purposes. It makes sure an animal mates with a partner of the same species. Mammals from different species cannot usually breed together and produce healthy young. The courtship also lets each partner check the health and strength of the other. If one of them is sick, then breeding may not be successful.

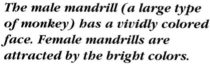

The male mandrill (a large type of monkey) has a vividly colored face. Female mandrills are attracted by the bright colors.

Many predators live solitary lives. The male and female live and hunt in separate areas. They come together only for a brief time to court and mate, then they go their separate ways again. This pair of tigers (left) will be together for only a week or two.

MATING

For a new life to begin, a microscopic tadpole-shaped sperm cell from the male must join with a pinpoint-sized egg cell from the female. This joining is called fertilization. Male and female mammals must join to mate. Their reproductive organs are shown on the right. To mate, the male places his penis into the female's vagina. He releases fluid containing sperm into her body. The sperm cells pass through her womb, and one fertilizes an egg, which begins its development into a baby.

Male mammals may have to battle against rivals to win the right to mate with females. Bull (male) elephant seals have huge, noisy struggles on the breeding beach, roaring and biting and slashing each other. Sometimes they are badly wounded and even die. Or they may roll or stamp on the baby elephant seals nearby and crush them to death.

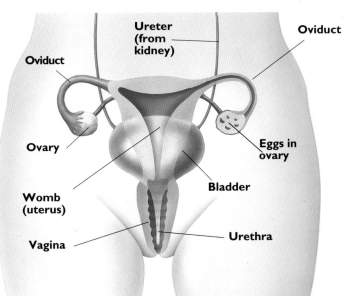

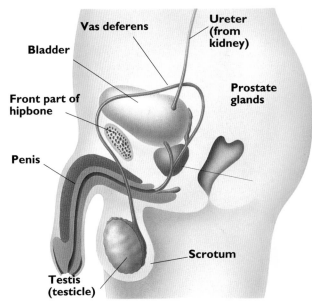

The main female reproductive organs are the two ovaries and the womb (uterus). The ovaries make egg cells, which travel to the womb along tubes called oviducts. If a sperm fertilizes the egg cell, it settles in the womb and begins to grow into a baby. The baby is born through the vagina.

The main male reproductive organs are the two testes and the penis. The testes make millions of sperm cells in a fluid called semen. During mating, the sperm pass along the vas deferens and through the penis, into the female's body. The prostate glands add fluids to nourish and stimulate the sperm.

◆ GROWING UP

The way mammals begin their lives is unique in the animal world. The young do not develop in an egg like a bird, or hidden under a log like a worm. They are warm, well nourished, and protected inside the mother's body. Even after the babies are born, most mammal parents look after the young until they can care for themselves.

PREGNANCY

Pregnancy, the time when a mother is carrying her young inside her, is very demanding. The mother needs extra food to help nourish herself and the growing babies. Yet she gradually becomes heavier and less agile. Many pregnant females rest and hide for much of this time, living on reserves of body fat.

MOTHER ALONE

Some babies are raised by only their mother. The female polar bear digs a den in snow or among rocks, and gives birth to one, two, or three cubs. She lives on her stored body fat and feeds the cubs on her milk. The family does not emerge from the den for three months. The mother-and-babies family unit is the most common arrangement among mammals.

Mammals are unique – they feed their young on milk made in the mother mammal's breasts, on her chest or belly (right). The babies suck the milk from rounded holes called nipples. It provides all their nourishment for the first weeks and months of life.

PREGNANCY

These are some average mammal gestation (pregnancy) periods, from the time of mating to the time the baby is born.

African elephant
660 days

Gray whale
390 days

Human
280 days

Fruit bat
180 days

Raccoon
65 days

Rabbit
30 days

Rat
23 days

TWO'S COMPANY

Marmosets are small South American monkeys. The babies are usually cared for by both mother and father. This two-parent family is relatively uncommon among mammals, though many humans are brought up this way.

Barbary macaque monkeys live in large groups called troops. The babies are cared for, cuddled, and carried by many members of the troop, including males.

The platypus and the two species of echidna (spiny anteater) are unusual mammals because they lay eggs with shells, like birds and reptiles. They are called monotremes, or egg-laying mammals. After the babies hatch, the mother feeds them on milk, like other mammals.

Many mammals, such as these badgers, dig a hole or construct a nest, in which they rear their young. The parent keeps the nest clean, and brings fresh bedding (grasses and leaves) for cleanliness and warmth. Badgers clean out the nest chamber and other parts of their sett (the tunnel system) almost every day.

The tiny newborn kangaroo is pink, hairless, blind, and barely an inch long. It "swims" through its mother's fur using its paddle-like arms, from her birth opening to the safety of her pouch.

LACTATION

The time period when a mother feeds her young on milk is called lactation. As the young grow stronger and more able to look after themselves, their mother stops feeding them milk, and they start eating solid food.

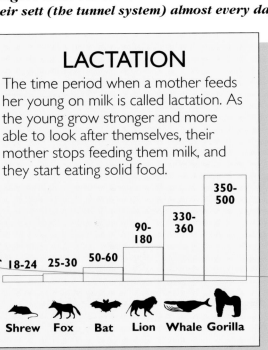

Days of Lactation

Shrew	Fox	Bat	Lion	Whale	Gorilla
18-24	25-30	50-60	90-180	330-360	350-500

Kangaroos, koalas, and wombats are marsupials, which breed in a different way to other mammals. Their babies are born tiny and only partly formed. They crawl through the mother's fur to her marsupium, or pouch. Here they continue their development, until they are strong enough to leave.

THE END

A female lemming can rear six or seven sets of offspring in one year, with as many as eight young in each set. So why isn't the world full of lemmings?

SURVIVING THE COURSE

It might be, but the majority of lemmings do not live past one month. Many are eaten at a very early age by foxes, hawks, and other creatures. Some lemmings freeze in icy weather, or die from starvation. Also, lemmings have a short lifetime naturally. By nine months, old age sets in!

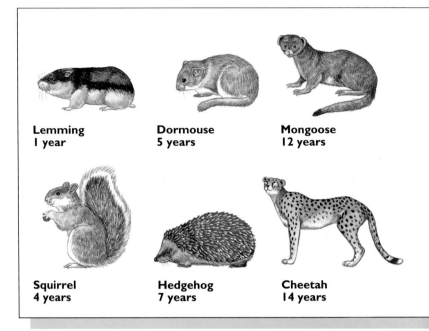

Lemming
1 year

Dormouse
5 years

Mongoose
12 years

Squirrel
4 years

Hedgehog
7 years

Cheetah
14 years

GROWING OLD

What is growing old? Bodies are complicated "living machines." But, like the machines we build, they do not last forever. The body's parts gradually wear out. An old lemming becomes weaker and more frail. Its senses fade, and its reactions slow down. It is thus even less likely to escape a predator's claws and teeth.

As a mammal becomes old, its body gradually changes. Some of the results of the ageing process are shown here. They are due to increasing wear and tear, and being unable to keep up with repair and renewal.

Lungs go stiff and are less efficient at taking in air

Hearing is dull and fades

Eyesight becomes less clear

Blood vessels harden and become blocked

Skin wrinkles and cracks

Fur goes brittle and coarse and falls out

Heartbeats are slower and weaker

Muscles weaken and tire more easily

Bones weaken and go brittle

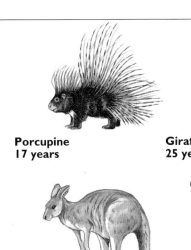

**Porcupine
17 years**

**Giraffe
25 years**

**Gorilla
40 years**

**Human
75 years**

**Kangaroo
20 years**

**Grizzly bear
35 years**

**Dugong
60 years**

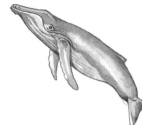

**Humpback whale
80 years**

Bigger mammals tend to live the longest. There are enormous variations, however. A baby wildebeest may be eaten by hyenas minutes after birth, or live a full 20 years. Here are approximate life-spans for mammals in their natural surroundings.

BENEFITS OF AGE

It's not all bad news for an older mammal. Some mammals rely on older members of the group for their "animal wisdom." In a herd of elephants, the leader is the oldest female. She is known as the matriarch.

The matriarch may be 50 years old or more. Using her knowledge, she guides the herd to water, pastures, and resting places. If danger approaches, she decides whether the herd should attack or retreat.

In Japan, macaque monkeys (left) have learned to wash their food in water, to get rid of sand and dirt. Young monkeys see the older ones doing this and copy them. This is a fairly new behavior – macaques have only recently been seen doing this – but it is now being passed from one generation to the next.

THE CONTINUING STRUGGLE

Nature is not kind, however. Predators are always ready for an easy meal, waiting to pick off the old, young, and sick. After they have eaten, even the bones crumble and disappear into the soil. Another body has lived and died.

A matriarch elephant and her companion chase away an elephant from another herd. Elephants rarely forget their survival skills.

INDEX